TO *Elaine and Chuck*

ON THE OCCASION OF *your wedding shower*

DATE *July 18, 1992*

FROM *Paul & Nancy Joseph*

Always and Forever

A WEDDING TREASURY

COMPILED BY ANNETTE REYNOLDS

INSPIRATIONAL PRESS

NEW YORK

Copyright © 1985 Lion Publishing

All rights reserved. No part of this work may be reproduced or transmitted in any form or by any means, electronic or mechanical, including photocopying, recording, or any information storage and retrieval system, without permission in writing from the publisher. All requests for permission to reproduce material from this Work should be directed to Lion Publishing Corporation, 10885 Textile Road, Belleville, Michigan 48111.

Published in 1992 by
Inspirational Press
A division of LDAP, Inc.
386 Park Avenue South
New York, New York 10016

Inspirational Press is a registered trademark of LDAP, Inc.

Published by arrangement with Lion Publishing plc, Herts, England, and Lion Publishing Corporation, Belleville, Michigan.

ISBN: 0-88486-060-4

Compiled by Annette Reynolds

Acknowledgments

Photographs by Ace Photo Agency, page 10; Alan Bedding, pages 34–35; Paul Craven, page 24; Sonia Halliday Photographs: Sonia Halliday, page 29, Sister Daniel, pages 18–19, 37; Lion Publishing: David Alexander, page 17 and endpapers, Jon Willcocks, pages 30–31, 40; S. & O. Mathews, pages 9, 32, 43; Jon Reynolds, page 23; Mick Rock, pages 14, 26–27; John Williams, cover; ZEFA, pages 13, 20, 38, 44

Bible quotations from *Good News Bible*, copyright 1966, 1971 and 1976 American Bible Society, published by Bible Societies/Collins, except those on pages 8, 12 and 21, which are from *Revised Standard Version*, copyright 1946 and 1952, second edition 1971, Division of Christian Education, National Council of the Churches of Christ in the USA

Extracts from the Marriage Service in *The Alternative Service Book 1980* are reproduced by permission of the Central Board of Finance; extracts from *An Australian Prayer Book* by permission of the Standing Committee of the Church of England in Australia; extract from *The Broadman's Minister's Manual* by Franklin M. Seger, Broadman Press, Nashville, Tennessee; extracts from *A Marriage Service For You* by Robert J. Peterson copyright © 1977 used with permission of CSS Publishing Company, Lima, Ohio; extracts from *The Methodist Service Book* by permission of the Methodist Conference; extracts from *Orders and Prayers for Church Worship* by permission of The Baptist Union

Other copyright material as follows: James Dobson, *Man to Man About Women*, Coverdale House Publishers Ltd, 1976, page 30; Jack Dominian, *Make or Break*, SPCK, 1984, pages 11, 15, 30, 33, 36, 39; Joyce Huggett, *Growing Into Love*, IVP, 1982, page 11; extracts from C. S. Lewis, *Mere Christianity*, Fontana Books, 1955 and *The Four Loves*, Fontana Books, 1963, reproduced by permission of Curtis Brown Ltd, London, pages 21, 36; John Powell, *The Secret of Staying in Love*, Argus Communications, a division of DLM, Inc., Allen, Texas 75002, 1974, page 42; Michel Quoist, *The Christian Response*, Gill and Macmillan, 1965 and *Meet Christ and Live*, Gill and Macmillan, 1973, pages 12, 16, 18, 25; Robert Runcie, *The Times*, 1984, pages 25, 28, 41; Ulrich Schaffer, *Love Reaches Out*, Lion Publishing, 1976 and *A Growing Love*, Lion Publishing, 1978, pages 22, 30; Paul Tournier, *The Gift of Feeling*, SCM Press, 1981, page 27; Walter Trobisch, *I Married You*, IVP, 1971 and *Love is a Feeling to be Learned*, IVP, 1974, pages 8, 22, 28, 39; Sheldon Vanauken, *A Severe Mercy*, copyright © 1977 by Sheldon Vanauken, reprinted by permission of Hodder and Stoughton Ltd, 1979, page 35; Hugh C. Warner, *Daily Readings from William Temple*, Hodder and Stoughton Ltd, 1948, page 45; John White, *Eros Defiled*, IVP, 1977, page 15

Every effort has been made to trace and contact copyright owners. If there are any inadvertent omissions in the acknowledgments, we apologize to those concerned

Printed and bound in Italy

Introduction

Love is a precious gift. It is about caring and companionship, tenderness and understanding, sorrow and joy.

The love that deepens into a lifelong commitment is a love that is willing to grow and mature. Expressed in the promises of the wedding service, it is a love that is prepared to enter into a mutual covenant of care and companionship. For richer, for poorer, in sickness and in health, it is a love that does not stand still, that never gives up.

This book brings together the richness of prayers and promises from a range of different wedding services with words from the Bible and the insights of Christian writers. It is a book to treasure right through the years of marriage — a constant encouragement to live out the love and commitment expressed on your wedding day.

God has created us male and female to walk together, side by side. In marriage two individuals become one flesh, united in love, in purpose and in spirit.

A CONTEMPORARY SERVICE BASED ON THE LUTHERAN TRADITION

"This at last is bone of my bones and flesh of my flesh . . . Therefore a man leaves his father and his mother and cleaves to his wife, and they become one flesh."
THE BOOK OF GENESIS, CHAPTER 2

"'To become one flesh' means much more than just the physical union. It means that two persons share everything they have, not only their bodies, not only their material possessions, but also their thinking and their feeling, their joy and their suffering, their hopes and their fears, their successes and their failures. 'To become one flesh' means that two persons become completely one, body, soul, and spirit, and yet there remain two different persons."
WALTER TROBISCH

We praise you, Father, that you have made all things, and hold all things in being. In the beginning you created the universe, and made mankind in your own likeness: because it was not good for them to be alone, you created them male and female; and in marriage you join man and woman as one flesh, teaching us that what you have united may never be divided.
THE ALTERNATIVE SERVICE BOOK 1980

God in his love and goodness toward us has given us marriage to be a precious gift. Through this gift we can know the deepest human relationship . . .

A CONTEMPORARY SERVICE BASED ON THE LUTHERAN TRADITION

> "Man made in the image of God possesses an inate ability to give love, to receive love, to communicate with others, to co-operate with others. This free-flowing love is expressed most intimately in marriage."
> JOYCE HUGGETT

> "The desire to be instantly understood and accurately responded to remains with us through life and is one of the clearest expressions of closeness and love between people."
> JACK DOMINIAN

Praise God, who has created courtship and marriage, joy and gladness, feasting and laughter, pleasure and delight, love, brotherhood, peace and fellowship.
THE METHODIST SERVICE BOOK

It is the will of Christ that in marriage the love of man and woman should be fulfilled in the wholeness of their life together, in mutual companionship, helpfulness and care.

THE METHODIST SERVICE BOOK

"Then the Lord God said, 'It is not good that the man should be alone. I will make a helper fit for him.'"
THE BOOK OF GENESIS, CHAPTER 2

"The love of a man and a woman gains immeasurably in power when placed under divine restraint."
ELISABETH ELIOT

"To love means to forget oneself entirely for the sake of another. It means to give oneself totally and freely in order to enrich another and to become one with him."
MICHEL QUOIST

*Almighty God, the Father of our Lord Jesus Christ
. . . Grant that these two persons may live together
in unity and love, seeking one another's welfare,
bearing one another's burdens, and sharing one
another's joys.*
ORDERS AND PRAYERS FOR CHURCH WORSHIP

It is given, that with delight and tenderness they may know each other in love, and, through the joy of their bodily union, may strengthen the union of their hearts and lives.

THE ALTERNATIVE SERVICE BOOK 1980

"We marry to make an alliance of mutual help and service, and as an expression of love. Intimacy in such a context is the seal of commitment. It is also a delicate communication of love and trust by which a man and a woman know each other ever more deeply."

JOHN WHITE

"Through the erotic encounter the husband is saying to his wife that he recognizes, wants and appreciates her as a person and similarly she reciprocates in her feelings... Thus in the depths of sexual intercourse are to be found the characteristics of thanksgiving, hope, reconciliation, sexual and personal affirmation. Love-making encompasses all these possibilities."

JACK DOMINIAN

O God, your generous love surrounds us, and everything we enjoy comes from you.
THE METHODIST SERVICE BOOK

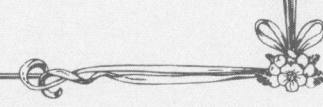

It is given, that they might have children and be blessed in caring for them and bringing them up in accordance with God's will, to his praise and glory.

THE ALTERNATIVE SERVICE BOOK 1980

"Children are a gift from the Lord; they are a real blessing."
PSALM 127

"God has brought me joy and laughter."
SARAH'S WORDS AFTER THE BIRTH OF ISAAC

"The Lord has filled my heart with joy; how happy I am because of what he has done!"
HANNAH'S PRAYER AFTER THE BIRTH OF SAMUEL

"Marriage is the foundation of true family life, and, when blessed with the gift of children, it is God's chosen way for the continuance of mankind and the bringing up of children in security and trust."
THE METHODIST SERVICE BOOK

"The most noble aspect of the human vocation is to be, with God, a creator . . ."
MICHEL QUOIST

We pray for this couple, that in their marriage all your will for them may be fulfilled; bestow upon them the gift and heritage of children; and endue them with all the gifts and graces needed for wise parenthood; through Jesus Christ our Lord. Amen
THE METHODIST SERVICE BOOK

Marriage is the symbol of God's unending love for his people, and of the union between Christ and his Church. So Saint Paul teaches that the husband must love his wife as Christ loved the Church, and that the wife must give due honour to her husband.

AN AUSTRALIAN PRAYER BOOK

"To love does not mean to seize the other for your own fulfilment but rather to give yourself to the other for his or her own fulfilment. You are ready for the experience of genuine love when your need, and especially your desire to give, is more compelling than your need and your desire to get..."

MICHEL QUOIST

We pray for your blessing on this man and this woman, who come before you as partners and heirs together of your promises. Grant that this man may love his wife as Christ loves his bride the Church, giving himself for it and cherishing it as his own flesh; and grant that this woman may love her husband and follow the example of those holy women whose praises are sung in the Scriptures.

THE ALTERNATIVE SERVICE BOOK 1980

It is a way of life that all should honour; and it must not be undertaken carelessly, lightly, or selfishly, but reverently, responsibly, and after serious thought.

THE ALTERNATIVE SERVICE BOOK 1980

"Trust in the Lord, and do good; so you will dwell in the land, and enjoy security. Take delight in the Lord, and he will give you the desires of your heart. Commit your way to the Lord; trust in him, and he will act."
PSALM 37

"Love as distinct from 'being in love' is not merely a feeling. It is a deep unity, maintained by the will and deliberately strengthened by habit, reinforced by (in Christian marriages) the grace which both partners ask, and receive, from God . . . 'Being in love' first moved them to promise fidelity: this quieter love enables them to keep the promise. It is on this love that the engine of marriage is run: being in love was the explosion that started it."
C. S. LEWIS

Heavenly Father, we thank you that in our earthly lives you speak to us of your eternal life: we pray that through their marriage this man and woman may know you more clearly, love you more dearly and follow you more nearly, day by day.
THE ALTERNATIVE SERVICE BOOK 1980

Will you love...

THE ALTERNATIVE SERVICE BOOK 1980

"Marriage needs love. It receives from love its fulfilment, its joy. Love is a gift to marriage. It provides marriage with the spirit of adventure, of never-ending expectation. Love is like the blood pulsing through the veins of marriage. It makes it alive."

WALTER TROBISCH

"Submission and love are two aspects of the same thing which is self-giving and self-sacrifice. And that is God's ideal for marriage and that is the secret of enduring happiness in married life."

JOHN STOTT

"Love is not the feeling
of a moment
but the conscious decision
for a way of life."

ULRICH SCHAFFER

God our Father, in your great love for mankind you have given us the gift of marriage; so bless these two persons as they pledge their lives to each other, that their love may evermore grow to be the true reflection of your love for us all; through Jesus Christ our Lord. Amen

AN AUSTRALIAN PRAYER BOOK

Will you comfort . . .

THE ALTERNATIVE SERVICE BOOK 1980

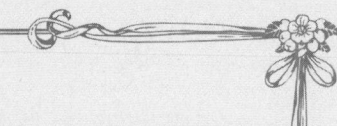

"Marriage . . . a union of two lives in which dependence and independence enhance each other, in which love comes to mean more than romance but certainly not less, and much more than mere unselfishness."
ROBERT RUNCIE

"Real love wants to share, to give, to reach out, it thinks of the other one, not itself."
WALTER TROBISCH

"There are two loves only, Lord,
Love of myself and love of you and of others,
And each time that I love myself,
It's a little less love for you and for others . . ."
MICHEL QUOIST

"O Divine Master, grant that I may not so much seek
to be consoled, as to console;
to be understood, as to understand;
to be loved, as to love."
FRANCIS OF ASSISI

Almighty God, Lord of the universe, all love, strength, and understanding come from you; so direct and govern us in body and soul that we may strive to live according to your word and to do everything that is agreeable to your will; through Jesus Christ our Lord. Amen
AN AUSTRALIAN PRAYER BOOK

Will you honour and protect . . .

THE ALTERNATIVE SERVICE BOOK 1980

"Love is patient and kind; it is not jealous or conceited or proud; love is not ill-mannered or selfish or irritable; love does not keep a record of wrongs; love is not happy with evil, but is happy with the truth. Love never gives up; and its faith, hope and patience never fail."
ST PAUL

"Love is action, not thought."
PAUL TOURNIER

Eternal God, true and loving Father, in holy marriage, you make your servants one. May their life together witness to your love in this troubled world; may unity overcome division, forgiveness heal injury, and joy triumph over sorrow.
THE ALTERNATIVE SERVICE BOOK 1980

Will you, forsaking all others, be faithful...

THE ALTERNATIVE SERVICE BOOK 1980

"Close your heart to every love but mine; hold no one in your arms but me. Love is as powerful as death; passion is as strong as death itself. It bursts into flame and burns like a raging fire. Water cannot put it out; no flood can drown it."

SONG OF SONGS, CHAPTER 8

"Cleaving means love, but love of a special kind. It is love which has made a decision and which is no longer a groping and seeking love. Love which cleaves is mature love, love which has decided to remain faithful — faithful to one person and to share with this one person one's whole life."

WALTER TROBISCH

"The great ideals, of which faithfulness is one, are great realities, not vague hopes . . . They need to grow as a harvest with patient cultivation."

ROBERT RUNCIE

Lord God, we give you praise and thanksgiving for all your gifts. We thank you that you created us, gave us the breath of life, and the ability to be one with another in faithfulness and in love.

A CONTEMPORARY SERVICE BASED ON THE
LUTHERAN TRADITION

I take you . . .
to have and to hold from this day forward

THE ALTERNATIVE SERVICE BOOK 1980

"Marriages are relationships which express the growing and changing aspirations of the couple. Growth and change are inescapable aspects of marriage . . . Husbands and wives come to know each other very well, accept what is good and encourage changes which promote the personality in its further development."
JACK DOMINIAN

"Love, even genuine love, is a fragile thing. It must be maintained and protected if it is to survive."
JAMES DOBSON

"Love comes as a gift; love must be renewed constantly."
ULRICH SCHAFFER

Most merciful and gracious God . . . Guide together this man and this woman in the way of righteousness and peace, that, loving and serving thee, with one heart and mind, all the days of their life, they may be abundantly enriched with the tokens of thy everlasting favour, in Jesus Christ our Lord. Amen

THE TRADITIONAL PRESBYTERIAN SERVICE

I take you...
for better, for worse, for richer, for poorer

THE ALTERNATIVE SERVICE BOOK 1980

"I know what it is to be in need, and I know what it is to have plenty. I have learned the secret of being content in any and every situation, whether well fed or hungry, whether living in plenty or in want."
ST PAUL

"Take heed, and beware of all covetousness; for a man's life does not consist in the abundance of his possessions."
LUKE'S GOSPEL, CHAPTER 12

"Marriage is a companionship which involves mutual commitment and responsibility. You will share alike in the responsibilities and the joys of life. When companions share a sorrow the sorrow is halved, and when they share a joy the joy is doubled."
THE BROADMAN'S MINISTER'S MANUAL

"The essential feature of marriage is the presence of a relationship between a man and woman. This relationship is first and foremost a sustaining experience. This sustaining is social, emotional, sexual, intellectual and spiritual."
JACK DOMINIAN

Eternal God, we pray that this man and woman will find through your grace, the power to fulfil their vows, and live together in love and harmony all the days of their life. Guide them through the difficult times, and give them a love that will deepen day by day, and year by year.
A CONTEMPORARY SERVICE BASED ON THE PRESBYTERIAN TRADITION

I take you . . .
in sickness and in health

THE ALTERNATIVE SERVICE BOOK 1980

"Two are better off than one, because together they can work more effectively. If one of them falls down, the other can help him up."

THE BOOK OF ECCLESIASTES, CHAPTER 4

"You can give without loving, but you cannot love without giving."

AMY CARMICHAEL

"Love not only begets love, it transmits strength."

SHELDON VANAUKEN

Father of love and mercy, pour out your grace upon this man and this woman and give them the power of your Spirit, so that they may fulfil with pure hearts and steady faith the vows made here today. Grant them courage for times of testing, endurance for times of trial, strength for times of weakness, but above all a constant love to knit together the heights and depths they will know.

A CONTEMPORARY SERVICE BASED ON THE
LUTHERAN TRADITION

To love and to cherish, till death us do part

THE ALTERNATIVE SERVICE BOOK 1980

"To love at all is to be vulnerable. Love anything, and your heart will certainly be wrung and possibly broken. If you want to make sure of keeping it intact, you must give your heart to no one . . ."
C. S. LEWIS

"The important thing is that love can go on growing until the last moment of our lives and has no limitations . . ."
JACK DOMINIAN

Almighty God, giver of life and love, bless this couple whom you have joined in holy matrimony. Grant them wisdom and devotion in the ordering of their common life that each may be to the other a strength in need, a counsellor in perplexity, a comfort in sorrow, and a companion in joy.
A CONTEMPORARY EPISCOPAL SERVICE

With my body I honour you

THE ALTERNATIVE SERVICE BOOK 1980

"Love longs for the physical expression, deepens it and makes it meaningful and precious. Through the physical surrender to each other, the lovers renew again and again their wedding vow."

WALTER TROBISCH

". . . sexual intercourse has such a rich potential to activate human love that only a continuous and exclusive relationship such as marriage can do full justice to it."

JACK DOMINIAN

Eternal God, we thank you for life, its wonder and mystery. We thank you for the capacity to share love with one another, and know the joys of that gift you gave us, when you created us in your own image.

A CONTEMPORARY NON-DENOMINATIONAL SERVICE

All that I am I give to you

THE ALTERNATIVE SERVICE BOOK 1980

"Marriage is a life-long union in which a man and a woman are called so to give themselves in body, mind, and spirit, and so to respond, that from their union will grow a deepening knowledge and love of each other."
AN AUSTRALIAN PRAYER BOOK

"Marriage . . . two people making a present of their whole lives to each other, so as to give each other unlimited scope to grow in mutual encouragement."
ROBERT RUNCIE

Blessed Lord, the author and giver of all good things, in whom is fulness of joy, send down your blessing, we beseech you, upon your servants whom you have joined as man and wife. Surround them with your good gifts. Bless them in each other, and both in the knowledge of Christ your Son our Lord.
Amen
THE METHODIST SERVICE BOOK

All that I have I share with you

THE ALTERNATIVE SERVICE BOOK 1980

"My emotions are the key to me. When I give you this key, you can come into me, and share with me the most precious gift I have to offer you: myself."
JOHN POWELL

"Love seeks one thing only: the good of the one loved. It leaves all the other secondary effects to take care of themselves. Love, therefore, is its own reward."
THOMAS MERTON

"The more he cast away, the more he had."
JOHN BUNYAN

Almighty Father, giver of life and love, look in favour on all who are made one in marriage, and especially on these your servants as they enter into their new life together. In your love deepen their love; strengthen their wills to keep the promises they have made; that they may live to your glory and to the good of mankind; through Jesus Christ our Lord.
Amen
AN AUSTRALIAN PRAYER BOOK

Those whom God hath joined together let no man put asunder.
THE BOOK OF COMMON PRAYER

'Jesus said to them . . . "But in the beginning, at the time of creation, 'God made them male and female,' as the Scripture says. 'And for this reason a man will leave his father and mother and unite with his wife, and the two will become one.' So they are no longer two, but one. Man must not separate, then, what God has joined together."'
THE GOSPEL OF MARK, CHAPTER 10

"This union should be, and is meant to be, an expression of a spiritual union so complete that it must be lifelong."
WILLIAM TEMPLE

Almighty and most merciful God, who hast now united this man and this woman in the holy estate of matrimony, grant them grace to live therein according to thy Holy Word. Strengthen them in constant fidelity and true affection toward each other. Sustain and defend them amidst all trials and temptations, and help them so to pass through this world in faith toward thee, in communion with thy holy Church, and in loving service one of the other, that they may enjoy forever thy heavenly benediction.

THE TRADITIONAL LUTHERAN SERVICE